POEMS FROM A BLACK GI 1974

LARRY BARTLETT SR.

Fulton Books
Meadville, PA

Published by Fulton Books 2024

ISBN 979-8-89221-414-8 (paperback)
ISBN 979-8-89221-415-5 (digital)

Printed in the United States of America

Acknowledgments

I would like to thank the following people who have helped me in the inspiration on this work of poetry. First is Mr. Jon Loff back in 1974—who was my first editor and my college Black literature professor at Allegany College of Cumberland, Maryland, and who gave me invaluable guidance. Second would be my wife, Pat, and my children Crystal and Larry Jr. for always having my back. And finally to Larry and Becky Gee for their inspiration in convincing me to share these poems to the world.

In memorial to my son Corey Shane (gone to soon) and my two best friends and brothers in life—Terry L. Pope and Barry W. Page—for always believing in me.

Music

Sitting here with my head feeling bad,
Everything's running through my mind,
Some are happy; most are sad.

Bad music reflects what I feel;
It opens my soul and mind
To the world that's real.

Music echoes every thought
By the way I live and the way I walk,
And sometimes shows even in my talk.

Let the music take your mind;
You'll see what I mean
To experience whatever you find.

When I'm gone, some will smile; others cry.
But I'm always jamming to bad music
At record sessions, getting high.

Say There, Lady

Say there, lady, I'm back in town.
What you been doing for yourself?
Tell me what's going down.

Say there, lady, I've heard the news,
You're four months pregnant,
And your rent is due.

Say there, lady, I'm doing fine.
I think about you a lot;
You're always on my mind.

Say there, lady, sit and rap awhile.
That frown isn't beautiful
Let me see you smile.

Say there, lady, I know it's rough.
It's a cold world out there,
Black Women have to be tough.

Say there, lady, wipe away those tears.
Keep your head high,
Show the world no fears.

Say there, lady, I'm a strong Black man.
I need a strong Black woman
To help me make a stand.

Say there, lady, it's going to be a long fight.
Black men, Black women together
Fight for equal rights.

Black Women, Black Women

Black women, Black women
Stand and spread the word
You've been quiet too long
It's time you were heard.

Black women, Black women
No more Aunt Jemima grins
Get out of that white kitchen
Go stand with your men.

Black women, Black women
Stop being treated like everyone's fool
Blacks need to be educated
Get your mind together, sister, stay in school.

Black women, Black women
Stop being the object of neglect
Strike back at this white world
Get up! Gain some RESPECT.

Black women, Black women
With your huge AFRO atop your head
Mean more to your men
Than just being good in bed.

Black women, Black women
Rear my black daughters and sons
Teach them to die for what they believe
And never fear the white bigot's gun.

Black women, Black women
You're a golden-brown queen
With such black beauty
The world has never seen.

White women, White women
Oh yes! You're blonde and fine
But you'll never truly understand
The workings of a Black man's mind.

Black women, Black women
Yes! You've almost reached your peak
Now stand my beautiful Black sisters
It's your turn to SPEAK.

May My Soul Rest in Hell

I remember as a child
I never listened to my parents
I always ran wild.

Never had time to go to school
I was out running the streets
You'd find me somewhere shooting pool.

I got my education out on the streets
I was known as Mr. Badass
Had the reputation as the very best thief.

I look back on my life, and it's a shame
How I wasted all the years in the streets
Playing all those jive hustling games.

I've now realized all the mistakes I've made
And I'll carry those heavy burdens
To my grave.

I pray that my son won't sit behind these walls
To look through the cold black bars
And long, dingy halls.

I now leave this world, with nothing left to tell
And I pray to God tonight
MAY MY SOUL REST IN HELL!

Saturday Morning Jones

Had a rough time last night,
Didn't pull a bitch
Got into a fight.

Shooting smack and drinking wine,
Helluva combination,
Fucks up your mind.

Saturday morning, trying to recover,
Roll a joint, brother.
Shit, I'll smoke another.

Feel too bad for a bite to eat,
Got out of bed,
And hit the street.

Damn, Jones is coming down,
Can't find a soul,
Not a pusher around.

Need something for my head
Find it quick
Shit, nigger give me a fix.

Pusher man coming out his door,
Look out motherfuckers,
I'll get "out there" some more.

Smoked a joint, got my kicks,
No time for bullshit, Brother,
I need a fix.

Smack now running through my veins,
Eating my life
Destroying my brain.

This dope giving me a one-side bought
It's too late now
Just nodded OUT!

World of Darkness

Looking out the window
There is no light
Never knowing if it is
Day or night.

Darkness surrounds me
Like an iron-covered fist
Never seeing anything
So I don't know what I miss.

I've learned to love the darkness
It brings me peace of mind
I see through things
Others can't find.

Right on for the darkness
And praise the night
Maybe one day soon
Others will see the light.

Actually, the whole world is blind
Everyone running in a daze
Not knowing the truth
Never looking to find.

One day soon the great light will shine
Everyone will stop and say
"It was their fault, not mine."

Thoughts

Sitting on the end of a bed
Music flowing through the air
Flashing lights of thoughts going through my head.

Had a damn good time today
Ran a game on a bitch
And I think she wants to play.

The music is taking my mind to far-off places
Longing to be home
And surrounded by familiar faces.

The music that is playing is about to end
Damn, man
When will I see my girl again.

But to hell with it, I'll be able to stand
Not much longer to go
To put up with the bullshit from the man.

Damn the music sure sounds good
Herbie Hancock jamming away
Doing it to death like I knew he would.

Thoughts attack me like drops of rain
Some heavy ideas and wisdom
Running through my brain.

People living their lives in a stupid daze
Letting all the joys of life
Pass by them in so many ways.

But I'm going to live the life I love
And love the life I live
Until they look over my body
And pronounce me dead.

In God We Trust

I've never read the Bible,
But I know what's inside.
I feel it in my heart, soul, and mind.

I know there is an Almighty above
Looking over all Black people
And sending his love.

We send him our praise each Sunday morning,
But Black soldiers die
And there is no warning.

God's Black children kicked aside
While God's White children
Say, "Die, nigger, die."

Big white churches tower the skies
People inside, bullshit themselves
Using God as their alibi.

Don't need church, not to be a sinner.
Check out the ministers
They're the deepest in it.

People use church like a storefront window,
Always looking inside
Never buying what's in it.

Black's struggle for freedom
Definitely a must.
All Black people saying, *In God we trust.*

The Things I See

The things I see can never be real for me
I see brothers trying to be fly
White dudes with their heads way up high
I see people of all kinds trying to be cool
Thinking they're living up to this so-called society's rules.

The things I see can never be real for me
Some dudes have their heads together and really know what
    is going down
Others are bullshitting themselves just playing the part of a
    circus clown
I see war, I see hate, and I see love
It's all going to come down to the man up above.

The things I see can never be real for me
I see young brothers trying to be hip
Their smoking dope, giving dap, and talking shit
The world around me is all the same
The people with the money playing their jive racist games.

The things I see can never be real for me
I go through mental changes every day
Being hassled by the man in the blue uniform, putting up
    with his bullshit games
Some people around me are not Black or White
I look into their minds and see that they know what is right.

The things I see can never be real for me
I see Turks who are proud and strong
I see Americans degrading these people all day long

I see young Black sisters and brothers growing up in the land
    of the free
All the time, being told, "Get back, nigger. You're not as good
    as me."

The things I see can never be real for me
I see dudes who claim they are your friend
Their just backstabbers doing things that will benefit them
I hear the nightly prayers that my mother sends
I see brothers rapping to my lady, and they will try to claim
    they are my best friend.

The things I see can never be real for me
I feel that a change is going to come
When everyone is united and becomes one
I won't see the changes in my lifetime
Because too many people in my world still have a closed mind.

The things I see can never be real for me
As time goes on and each day that I last
I look ahead to my future and back at my past
I know that I've found myself and I know who I am
And every day I try to pass my knowledge on to my fellow man.

Maybe someday the things that I see will be real
If everyone learns to keep their head to the sky
And follow God's will.

THE END

Out There!

I'm just as high as I want to be.
A room full of freaky dudes
Just as high as me.

Everyone digging the sounds
Outside this room
A whole lot of shit going down.

Right now I don't give a damn
Bust me "MAN"
To hell with "UNCLE SAM."

My president even quit
So why should I
Give a shit?

Maybe later I might care
But right now my head is bad
And I'm just out there.

Ode to a Legionnaire

Niggers stand 'round a bar,
Ignorant and happy,
They won't go far.

All playing "dumb nigger game,"
Too goddamn stupid
To come in from the rain.

Try to pull a bitch,
Got my rap together,
Don't say I ain't shit.

Just lay and scope the scene,
Mothers miss the point.
You know what I mean?

Think I'm strange since been gone?
I'm an individual
All day, all night long.

Super Cool

Look at me, I'm really cool
You can't tell me shit
I'm no one's fool.

I smoke dope and drink wine
Have plenty of bitches
They're all super fine.

Carry a "38" on my hip
I don't bullshit around
I take no lip.

Drive nothing but brand new "Hogs"
For personal bodyguards
Two German shepherd dogs.

All my clothes are tailor-made
Wear a big gold watch
Rings on my fingers with stones of Jade.

Look at me I'm really cool
You can't tell me shit
I'm no one's fool.
MAYBE!

Got No Time

Got no time to run and sing,
Get up, Black people
It's time to do our thing.

Got no time for "Sanford and Son,"
Get up, Black people
And grab a gun.

Got no time to skin and grin,
Get up, Black people
Stand and be men.

Got no time for soap opera dreaming,
Get up, Black people
With your voices screaming.

Got no time, taught with two-hand books,
Get up, Black people
Get educated, take a new look.

Got no time for jiving and jeffin',
Get up, Black people
It's time we go steppin'.

Only got time for modesty and truth,
Get up, Black people
Show Whitey our roots.

Oh Say Can You See

Oh say can you see the dawns early light
What is the destiny of this world
Who is to help in the BLACK MAN'S PLIGHT?

What is the deal on this twilight gleaming
White people living secure
While Blacks are still dreaming.

Red, white, and blue trimmed in the shining gold
A black man stripped of his heritage
Say, man! This shit's getting old.

Your eagle with its head of white
A symbol for the white majority
A buzzard stands for niggers
Your so-called low-class minority.

I have no flag or anthem to sing
You've denied me equal education,
Peace of mind, and material things.

I now have the RED, BLACK, and GREEN
The colors from my motherland
I know what each one means.

Red is for the millions of black lives lost
But the system doesn't care
As long as it is not at the government's cost.

Black is for all my people
Just longing for the day
When we stand as tall as any steeple.

Green represents the land on which I stand
The color of the great American dollar
Which won't let me be a man.

Oh say can you see the dawns early light
Black people coming on strong
Not long to go we will soon make it right.

Because I'm Black

Keep your head up in the crowd
Stand up and be a proud Black Man
Let all Black voices be loud.

Just because my skin is Black
I'm forced to wear hand-me-down clothes
And live in rat-infested shacks.

I only want the chance to be a man
After all, my ancestors were forced
To come build this free land.

I've been stripped of my manhood
For groups of years
Suffered through agony, pain, and tears.

No more lynchings and senseless killings
Everything could get together
But both Black and White have to be willing.

So you think that you're really hip
You been hanging out with the big boys
Claiming you're into a lot of shit.

Your mind is wrapped up in a lot of your own false dreams
It's time to get your head together man
And check out the real scene.

You try to copy others because you think their way is cool
Only those who are individuals survive
The rest are fools.

    LARRY BARTLETT SR.

First, you've got to search your own mind
It's a very heavy trip
To realize what you find.

I'll no longer be the good house nigger
Showing those pearly whites
Watch out, world, this Black man's going to stand up for his
      rights.

Three young Black children grow up hungry to your tune
While you waste the money
By sending three White men to the moon.

You send me off to fight wars in far-off lands
And when I return home
You refused to let me be a man.

The time is here and the time is now
For all Black people to stand
And be united and proud.

THE END

About the Author

Larry Bartlett is originally from Cumberland, Maryland, born in 1952, and graduated from Allegany High School in 1970. He entered the US Air Force in 1971 and served until 1975. He worked as a railroad conductor for CSX for thirty-five years before retiring in 2012. He now lives with his wife, Patricia, in Fairborn, Ohio. The year 1974 was the first time that I have written any poems. I attribute it to a spiritual awakening in my soul to living in a foreign country and discovering my place in the world.